SIMPLE RELATIONSHIP WISDOM

Secrets to a Happy Relationship

Rita Panahi, L.Ac., Dipl.O.M.

ISBN: 978-0-9996648-5-8

First Edition: Dec 2020

10% of all author royalties are donated to the poor

DEDICATED TO:

My family

Nature

My teachers

To the Reader

The contents of this book are intended to inspire you to experience healthier and more harmonious relationships in your life. All relationships face challenges at one point or another, and we need support, especially during those times, to help us bring about more closeness rather than distance and separation.

This book is simple, concise, and filled with wisdom. It is a perfect daily go-to resource to realign you with the key elements of a successful relationship. However, it is not meant to substitute any form of therapy or counseling that might be required.

May it guide you to greater happiness and joy in all of your relationships!

Relationships aren't made in heaven.
We see heaven in our relationships.

TABLE OF CONTENTS

INTRODUCTION

Relationships can be heaven on earth—or just the opposite. It depends on how we approach them and the quality of effort we put in.

Just as batter will not yield a delicious cake without the right ingredients added, so too, a relationship cannot have the sweetness of love and harmony unless we put in the right elements every day. To bake a delicious cake, we require certain staple ingredients; but if we add even a small amount of an ingredient such as ground pepper into the batter, the overall taste will dramatically change to reflect it.

Furthermore, in the same way that we cannot be physically healthy while eating all the wrong foods, we cannot create a healthy relationship by putting in all the wrong elements (or none at all).

Relationships are a part of our daily lives. Their quality can impact our mind, emotions, and even our physical health tremendously.

This book is intended to give you the key ingredients, in a straightforward format, for creating love and harmony in your life and all your relationships. Though the word *partner* is used frequently throughout the book, it can be substituted for *child, parent, spouse, girlfriend, boyfriend, friend,* or *colleague* as applies to you. While we get busy taking care of all of our responsibilities, it is easy to forget about caring for our relationship. In those moments when you feel run down or aggravated and you are struggling in your relationship, pick up this book and open it to any chapter to recall the element that might be lacking in the moment.

Any time we have conflict in our relationship, our peace and happiness will be disturbed. However, if we follow the recipe, we can often bake a pretty amazing cake. We simply need the right ingredients!

I hope you will be inspired to bring sweetness and harmony back into your relationship.

Plant the seeds for a happy and healthy relationship in order to harvest its sweet fruits in due time.

1

Business Deal

People tend to handle their relationships as they do their work. Some hate their work but continue doing it because they see no other option. Some love their work and dedicate themselves entirely to it. Others do their work half-heartedly, seeking other projects on the side to distract themselves from their unhappiness and all the while wishing they could find a way out. Still others pretend they are happy where they are but secretly send out resumes so they can transition at the first viable opportunity.

When sincere love is missing, whether in our work or relationships, our performance is half-hearted. We can try to convince ourselves or others to the contrary by pretending to be fully present, but sooner or later, our true feelings surface and achieving success becomes a strenuous uphill climb. Love is the foundation for anything that has a chance of truly succeeding. It is through love that we have the desire to put in the effort required.

It may happen in a relationship that one partner is fully present and committed and the other is only pretending to be so, wishing for a way out whilst damaging the trust and integrity within the relationship. Sometimes this is a symptom of entering or staying in a relationship for the wrong reasons, with love hardly playing a role—for example, seeking independence from living with your parents, fulfilling the obligation of marriage due to family pressure, or being with someone because of their wealth, status, or appearance.

It is the joy that relationships bring that make them worthwhile and beautiful. It is the longing to be together and enjoy a shared life that allows the flower of love to blossom ever more radiantly.

If a relationship is entered into as a business deal, then various tactics are used to get the other to "hold up their end." The other is never loved or appreciated for who they are deep within but rather for what they can provide. And, not being valued, they become disposable. We rarely wish to invest in a disposable item.

The journey to true success in relationship comes by seeing the inner being of the person and loving them for it. It is through love that any effort becomes effortless. When love is present, you naturally want to give your hundred percent. If a relationship can be compared to a business deal at all, then it should be viewed as an investment of love. The more you invest in your relationship, the higher your returns will be. You need to be willing to invest in loving your partner. That is the only investment worthwhile when it comes to a relationship.

2

POWER VERSUS LOVE

Rather than providing an environment where love is shared, relationships often turn into a battleground.

There are two paths in life, and we have a choice as to which to take. One is the pursuit of power. The other is the cultivation of love.

When you see yourself as being on the opposite side of the court from someone, your goal is to defeat the opponent. When you see yourself as being on the same side, your goal is to work together towards a mutual vision.

We seek power when we want to boost our ego. The ego invariably sees itself as separate from others and fights to show its superiority. It seeks to be better than the other and lift itself higher. It sees separation and disparity. When our focus is to defeat and feel superior, the path we are following is that of power gain.

Society trains people's minds to desire victory, domination, and control, whether in spiritual matters, material gains, or relationships. It teaches us that power is equivalent to strength and the lack thereof is equivalent to weakness. However, on the path of love, unity is the sign of strength, and ego or separation is the sign of weakness.

Love comes from an open heart that sees itself as a team, as part of the other. The other's happiness brings happiness to those who are on the path of love. The sight of someone suffering or failing awakens compassion in those who are on the path of love. There is no "higher" and "lower."

The struggle between power and love is the foremost cause of conflict in relationships. Power never wants to bow down and feel like a loser. Apologizing makes it feel inferior. It demands to be served, to have the final word, to have things its way, and to be the boss. Love, on the other hand, sees the other at eye level and as a partner on the same team. If love sees the other losing, it feels they have both lost.

It's important to ask yourself if you are walking the path of love or the path of power in your relationship. False power is the path of the ego, of self-centeredness. True power is the path of love, care, and selflessness. For relationships to succeed, power needs to be put aside so that love has a chance to grow.

3

RECIPROCITY

A business deal is entered into with the intention of making a profit, even at the expense of the other. If this mindset is taken into our personal relationships, the balance between giving and taking—the balance of reciprocity—is lost. Sooner or later one person begins to feel resentful for giving more of themselves than is given by the other.

Entering into a relationship while thinking first about what you will get from it, whether it be money, prestige, an attractive companion, information, or even love, will always leave you strategizing to take from the other in order to gain more and be on top. Usually the one taking more is caught up on the power path and the one giving more is following the path of love. No relationship can tolerate this imbalance for long. The two paths will often lead in opposite directions, leaving little chance for harmony.

People generally fall into two categories when it comes to relationships: givers and takers. Givers feel so abundant within that they overflow by giving to others, seeing them as an extension of themselves. Takers, on the other hand, seek to fill the sense of lack they feel within. They take when possible to fill the void and experience power. Even their act of giving has the underlying purpose of receiving in return, so that the giving is not coming from the heart but instead is a habitual tactic or conscious plan to gain at some future point.

Personal relationships, if entered into with the preconceived idea of some sort of profit to be won, cannot be maintained for very long. That is the mindset of power and lacks reciprocity, which is the key ingredient for success. Reciprocity is the essence of the beauty of love in a relationship. A true sign of love is when you want to be with someone because giving to them and making them happy fills you with happiness.

If we seek to learn from nature, we realize that it is always giving. The tree generously gives its fruits. The sun showers its light. The earth supports the seeds for food to grow. If both partners align with nature's example, then both are always giving to and hence receiving from each other. In this way, reciprocity exists and both partners feel joy in the relationship. However, without this balance, one of the partners feels depleted and unhappy—often, the one who is receiving less than they are giving.

To heal your relationship, be like a tree which offers all it has: shelter, fruit, and beauty. Let yourself be a vessel overflowing with love. When both partners give of themselves equally, the flow of the relationship is peaceful and joyful. Just as the left hand may take a heavy weight from the right to give it a moment to rest, so too, in a reciprocal relationship, one partner helps the other to reduce their burden and bring them more joy. Allow the give-and-take of your relationship to be balanced by putting aside selfishness and inviting more selflessness into your lives.

The sun and the moon
are showing you the dance of love
as they rotate around the earth,
each taking turns to show their beauty.

4

WATERING THE PLANT

What happens to a plant that isn't watered frequently? Unless it is a cactus, it will most likely shrivel and die.

This concept is simple, yet most people imagine that a relationship is immune to nature's laws, able to survive harsh treatment or even neglect. A relationship requires regular nourishment to thrive, in the form of love and attention.

People are like different species of plants. Some require a lot of sun exposure, pruning, and watering; others prefer watering only a few times a week; and yet others, like a cactus, thrive with minimal upkeep.

You have to know who you are bringing into your life (or already have in your life) and what their "care instructions" are. If you treat a delicate flower like a cactus, don't be surprised when it wilts. If you overwater a cactus, don't be surprised when it becomes waterlogged and rots.

If we aren't able to care for our partner according to their needs, the survival of the relationship becomes difficult down the line. So, in the same way that we take the time to learn how to properly nourish our plants, it's important to do the same with our partner.

As a relationship progresses, it's often assumed that our partner will continue giving us the same love as always while we focus on our work or other interests, without feeling the need to give them the attention or care we used to.

Suddenly we find the same plant that was once joyful and radiant is now drooping, having lost its vibrancy. We attribute the deterioration to the plant's own problems and fail to see the role that we played in it.

The nourishment we give each other in a relationship is what fills our hearts with even more love to give. Understand the needs of your partner, learn their "care instructions," and take the time to support their blossoming. On the path of love, their happiness adds to yours.

5

SUNSHINE

Kind words and compliments in a relationship are like sunshine for a plant; they make its flowers bloom and smile. On the other hand, excessive rain and storms will make the petals wither, the stems break, and the leaves droop. A relationship without warmth, affection, and love is like a day with no sunshine. The dreariness may be tolerated for a while, but eventually it will turn the relationship cold.

Consider a garden. It needs to be maintained by weeding, pruning, watering, and fertilizing the soil. Just as our plants will die if neglected, our relationship can end if we don't give it the maintenance it requires through our love, care, affection, and kindness.

By taking the necessary time to care for what we have, we can prevent ourselves from treating our partner as a valueless flower that can be easily allowed to wilt and then replaced by a new budding plant from the local garden center.

Rather than use-and-throw-away mentality, we need to develop the mentality of continually giving sunshine to our partner through our love. The light that we shine into our relationship is the happiness that we bring to our partner's heart through our care and affection. We bring warmth through our words and actions. Bringing happiness to others is living in the consciousness of divinity. When we see our relationship as our garden, we can shower it with divine energy, giving it priority, attention, care, and nourishment. We then see our garden blossom into a masterpiece, a garden of love.

6

PRESENCE

Time is often scarce in relationships. Running after money and climbing the career ladder can leave little time left over to spend with our partner, let alone be fully present with them during that time. Many give their partner only the crumbs of the free time they have, leaving a hole of longing and emptiness in the other's heart.

A key beauty of relationship is the quality time spent together and the activities and memories shared. Without that quality time, we may just as well be single.

Acquiring wealth—as important as it is for survival and comfort—can compete with the quality time and love that helps a relationship to grow and be sustained. As such, money and time can end up on opposite sides of the coin. We either end up having a lot of money but little time, or a lot of time but little money.

Time by itself, however, does not hold the same value if true presence is lacking. In other words, we can be in the same room with our partner and yet be occupied with our own thing—never connecting to them, never listening to their heart, and never talking about things that are on our mind.

Balancing money and time is important in a relationship, and alongside that, giving our true presence, undivided attention, and quality time. The greatest amount of money will not buy love nor quality time. It is one of our greatest and rarest assets that we take for granted.

Thirty minutes of giving our full attention and presence is more valuable than twenty-four hours of being physically but not emotionally or spiritually present with our partner.

We are on the earth for only a short period of time. Though money may come and go throughout our life, time will only decrease in quantity. Therefore, of the two, time is more precious.

Being present in that quality time is the greatest gift we can give to someone that we love.

You may have been married for ten years, but how many of those years did you truly spend being present with one another and being there for each other? How much of that time did you stop everything else to look at, listen to, and be with your partner and give them your full, undivided presence?

When our heart is truly open, we welcome our partner fully into our life and heart, giving them our most precious combination of resources—our time and presence.

Love is a decision.
Honesty is a decision.
Caring is a decision.
Our decisions form the foundation
of our relationship.

7

THE ART OF LISTENING

How can we find a solution to any of life's problems if we are not willing to listen, either to our partner or to our own mind and heart? Often, we come to a conclusion before we have heard our partner's take. Other times, we may walk away and choose not to listen to them at all. Yet other times, we may pretend like we are listening, but our mind is elsewhere as they speak to us.

Listening is about being receptive. It's about having the patience to hear something we may not like, be comfortable with, or even agree with at the moment. It's about being open.

We may think we are listening if we hear their words, but we may not be letting those words enter our heart and mind so that we can truly understand what they mean. Hearing merely allows the sound to enter our ears. Listening allows the words to enter our heart and mind with receptivity. If we are already deciding how to respond or shaking our head in disagreement while our partner is still speaking, we are closing the doors on receptivity.

True listening is an art. It's an openness that allows spoken words to enter our heart so that we can understand another person deeply. Even when anger, sadness, or frustration is expressed, through true listening with the heart and mind, we can understand the essence of what is being shared with us.

Oftentimes we become defensive and block our own ability to listen. Defensiveness is like a wall that we create between ourselves and our partner. It blocks true communication. Rather than solving a problem, it creates even more frustration and distance.

When you feel frustrated or you don't have the desire to listen to your partner, stop, take a few deep breaths, close your eyes, and feel your heartbeat with your hand. Remember that your time on earth and with each other is finite. They wouldn't be speaking if they weren't trying to share something with you. They may be speaking simply because they are alone and don't know how to express it other than speaking about what appears to be random events. They may be having a difficult time expressing themselves clearly. In such cases it is especially important to look beneath what is being said.

Give your partner thirty minutes of your time and listen with your heart, letting what they have to say sink in without reacting. Respond only once you feel you have let the words enter your heart and you understand the essence of what they are sharing. Practice listening deeply while being fully present and giving your undivided attention.

8

WORDS

Words are the wind that carry the ship of your relationship forward. Without words, there is little movement. With the wrong words, you can set your ship in the wrong direction or even straight into a storm. Constructive communication is critical in all relationships.

Communication happens on many levels. Words are one powerful aspect of it, but we also communicate through our tone, our silence, and our actions (or lack thereof).

We need to choose our words and the tone behind them carefully so that they bring closeness rather than conflict.

Letting our heart be an active participant in our dialogue with our partner ensures that the words come from the right place. After all, words are treasures of energy that we pass between each other. We need to think of their power before speaking.

As powerful as words are, silence is an equally powerful form of communication. Silence can demonstrate either respect or contempt. When we are silent in order to not interrupt our partner, we are displaying our respect for them. However, when we are silent with anger brewing within our heart, and we purposefully ignore our partner's need for communication, we create greater distance from them. This type of silence can leave a lot of room for assumptions and even more misunderstandings.

Ignoring someone, giving them the silent treatment, or walking away is the equivalent of a slap in the face or saying, "I don't care about what you have to say" or "You are unimportant to me."

Becoming defensive when communicating is a form of rebellion and also has undertones of, "I have no interest in what you have to say. I don't have to listen to you. I don't have any respect for you, your thoughts or feelings."

Just as the ocean's undercurrents may have the strength to change the direction of the waves on the surface, so too, words and silence carry undercurrents that can direct the relationship, either in the desired or opposite direction. We need to ask ourselves what it is that we are really communicating with our words and our silence and be mindful of the direction they are taking us.

9

TRUTH

Love requires seeing your partner as your teammate. Lying to them puts them in the position of an opponent. When they're no longer on your team in your heart and mind, love is pushed to the back seat. In the same way that you are more cautious and fearful around an enemy, you can't be in a state of openness and love when you lie to someone. The foundation of developing intimacy is trust. And honesty is the key ingredient of trust.

Many imagine that if they don't tell their partner a direct lie but simply withhold the truth, it's not considered a lie.

They believe that only spoken untruths are actual lies. They are deluding themselves. Within every relationship is an inherent energy, and although it cannot be seen, it has a very powerful presence. Some people refer to it as the soul or the energy field of the relationship. As humans, we are energy beings alongside our physical existence. We have an energy field surrounding us that has its own intelligence. This is the reason why we feel things, even if we are not conscious of what exactly it is that we are feeling or where the feeling is coming from in our environment. The ripples of peace and harmony are different than the ripples of discord and unease.

Generally, a person who lies is aware that they do it, even if it has become so habitual that they are not fully conscious of it while they are doing it. While they may feel justified in lying and keeping a secret from their partner, there is a knowingness of their soul deep within that is aware that doing so is wrong. The secret is like a poison that slowly breaks the peace and harmony within the relationship as it infiltrates and destroys the foundation of trust.

In the same manner, the soul of the person being lied to knows and feels the poison that has been injected into their relationship—even if never explicitly told that they are being lied to. The soul always knows. The energy field always knows. It may not know the precise details, but it knows. It is the same as unknowingly eating food that has gone bad; slowly the illness kicks in and the damage becomes worse and worse.

If the relationship's energy field is filled with lies and deception, it gradually destroys the foundation of the relationship. The peace, beauty, and harmony of the relationship are broken down.

Again, our partner doesn't need to be told that we have wronged them. Their soul already knows, even though they may not consciously be aware of it. And that inner knowingness is what will create unpleasant reactions and distancing in the relationship.

We enter into a relationship with one another to share and exchange love, ideas, and time. If we lie to each other, what are we then sharing? Fictional stories with no real meaning? When you lie to a person whom you claim to love, you are indirectly saying to them that they are not worth your honesty and that you love neither them nor yourself.

We may get so busy in life that we don't take the time to reflect on the consequences of our actions and instead only consider their short-term impact. We eat the pie now, not thinking about the calories we have to burn tomorrow. We spend the money now, not thinking of how hard we'll have to work to make it back. We lie to our partner now, not thinking that we will have to deal with the consequences of the lie—namely, destruction of trust and a deeply hurt heart.

A moment of deception can lead to a lifetime of regret. There's physical betrayal, of course—in the form of infidelity—but there is also betrayal of the soul of the partner and the soul of the relationship. Deception of any kind breaks the invisible threads that bind two people together and shatters the foundation of the relationship. Therefore, it's important to think twice before lying to your partner. Truth is a treasure. It is the rock that the relationship is built on. If you feel you have to lie, deeply consider the reason why. Whatever the reason is, consider removing it from your life, which will in turn remove the impetus to lie in the first place.

Words can be like arrows,

creating wounds in others

that take time to heal.

Or words can be like water,

washing away others' wounds.

10

GREENER GRASS

If we continually feel as though we are lacking something, we will keep searching for it. Our appetite may never be satiated. This concept may apply to any aspect of our life, from material things to relationships. When we feel full from within and are grateful for what we have, the desire to keep searching falls away. If we don't heal the core of our unhappiness within ourselves and our relationship, the chances that we will look for greener grass elsewhere increase substantially.

Looking for love or fun with someone else outside of the relationship may seem like a harmless short-term solution to our discomfort and unhappiness, but the wounds it leaves behind can harm our partner, whom we love, for a lifetime.

It's never easy to deal with challenges within our relationship, but unfaithfulness is like a mirage in the desert. We think we are seeing water ahead that will quench our thirst, yet once we reach the destination we realize there was really nothing there in the first place. Unfortunately, when it comes to relationships, walking towards that illusion destroys the heart of our partner—which instills a pain that can rarely be healed easily.

Before opening the door to the desire to seek happiness elsewhere, you need to look it directly in the eye and ask yourself whether you are contributing to finding a solution with your partner. Are you truly listening to your partner? What do you feel is missing in the relationship, and have you communicated it well to your partner? Are you stressed about something else and projecting it onto your partner? Are you feeling disempowered, looking to boost your ego through an outside source?

It is better to take the time to reflect deeply before taking steps that might ultimately destroy the relationship and leave a deep wound as a memory. Believing the grass is greener elsewhere is often a result of feeling lack within ourselves and our relationship.

Both men and women fall into the trap of searching outside their relationship for what they feel they are lacking. It is a human weakness. And for every man or woman who is unfaithful to their partner, there is another man or woman outside of the relationship who is supporting that infidelity. The lies multiply between our partner, the person we are having the affair with, and ultimately our own self.

Being unfaithful can happen on many levels. If our mind and heart begin to turn toward a person besides our partner, we have already begun the process. Our presence begins to shift to that other person; our energy, time, attention, and emotions soon follow. The resources we could be sharing with our partner in order to nourish our relationship are now given to someone else, depriving the one whom we have given our commitment to.

We have limited time, energy, and resources as human beings, as much as we would like to believe otherwise. Sharing those things elsewhere due to our own inner unhappiness or dissatisfaction only reduces what we can give our partner, which consequently creates more distance and makes us an emptier vessel within the relationship. Many times, we fail to see what we actually have with our partner because we don't take the time to look deep enough and give our true presence and care.

Before falling into the trap of searching for greener grass elsewhere—a trap that you might not be able to disentangle yourself from without destroying the relationship—you might consider reflecting deeply on your desires, the root of your unhappiness, and the long-term consequences your wandering heart might have on your life and your partner's life.

11

LOYALTY

Loyalty is the ability to keep focus. In a relationship, loyalty has to do with our ability to keep our focus on one person—our partner—and not let it wander, not only physically but emotionally and mentally as well. It is the nature of the mind to wander; but in order to reach a goal, we need focus, which ultimately can be defined as loyalty to the goal. Therefore, success within a relationship can only be achieved through focus and loyalty.

An unfocused mind brings a sense of insecurity to a relationship because we can never know where it will wander to and the temptations that will result from it. This instability keeps our partner on the edge, ruining the harmony and depth that the relationship needs to succeed.

Loyalty, on the other hand, brings a stability and groundedness that allows our partner to feel at peace.

If our goals have selfish roots, then loyalty in our relationship may be difficult. However, if our goals are centered on our partner and the relationship, it becomes a lot more effortless to keep our heart and mind focused on long-term visions of success. Loyalty allows a relationship to grow deep roots, forming a strong foundation as its shared visions and dreams reach for the sky.

12

DEALING WITH CONFLICT

Anyone can love another person when they are happy and peaceful. It is when challenges arise and inner wolves appear that maintaining our love and kindness becomes more difficult.

What do you do when you face difficulties? Do you go to a bar and drink? Do you fight? Do you look for greener grass? Do you bury yourself in work? Do you look for happiness outside your relationship to distract you? How do you deal with stress and conflict?

Conflicts are bound to happen in life, no matter how hard we try to avoid them. And how we deal with them leads to yet other consequences. In a relationship, the ability to deal with conflict sets the foundation of the future of the relationship and the potential for its success.

If we run away each time there is discord, the relationship is bound to fail. There are many exits we can use to run away from the discomfort we might experience during conflict. Some people may overeat or overdrink, some may literally walk out on the other person, some may choose infidelity as their escape, and some may hide themselves behind their work. Everyone has their learned habit of dealing with unpleasant circumstances or problems. Yet most of these unhealthy habits don't resolve anything.

Running away, giving the silent treatment and keeping our frustration hidden, or becoming defensive in response to conflict is bound to lead to the relationship failing. These tactics create a wall between two people. And a wall only creates a state of more distance and frustration where nothing can be resolved.

Receptivity to face conflicts head on takes strength. It also takes the ability to examine ourselves and our patterns.

When seeking a life partner, evaluating their ability to resolve conflicts can show you a lot about what to expect in your relationship.

Below are several important questions to ask before making long-term plans with a potential partner. If you are in a relationship already, these questions should shed more light on yourself or your partner's disposition to deal with challenges.

- How are your problem-solving skills?
- What do you do when there is a problem in your life?
- How do you handle stress?
- Do you quickly get defensive?
- Do you run away when there is a problem?
- Do you communicate about what's bothering you?
- Do you become abusive?

- Do you give up easily when faced with difficulties?
- Do you truly listen?
- Do you lie to avoid conflict?
- Do you overeat, drink, or do drugs to avoid problems?
- Do you own your contribution to the problem?

These questions should be asked about your partner as well as yourself. Many of them stem from key concepts mentioned throughout this book. Use those chapters as your focus to strengthen your unhealthy habits. If you are aware of your own weaknesses, you can work on them.

The choices you make today
have consequences you will need
to deal with tomorrow.
Choose wisely.

13

WEEDS OF THE PAST

Relationships don't end just because we have left the person, signed the divorce papers, or moved far away. The painful experiences we have had with our former relationships leave their mark on our heart and mind for many years after separation.

Without finding closure from our feelings, we move into a new relationship amidst the smell from an un-emptied garbage can. We may cover up the unpleasant odor for some time or pretend that it doesn't even exist, but after a while, we realize how it is polluting our fresh new relationship.

Whenever we enter into a new relationship while still carrying the remnants of an old one, we are unable to truly see the person we are with. We project our anger, fear, or sadness onto the person in front of us when in reality they may not be the cause of it.

The flower of a new relationship can't grow among the weeds of the past. The weeds only block our view from truly seeing and being present with our partner. We need to uproot those weeds in order to give our present relationship the fresh soil that it deserves and needs in order to blossom.

In the same way that we have rituals for birthday celebrations and weddings, we also need to perform rituals for ending relationships, whether through death or separation. For example, we can write a letter to our former partner expressing all of our pain, sadness, and anger as well as the happy memories. We don't need to send it to them, because this is simply a ritual for our own heart. We can take the letter and sit under a tree or somewhere in nature and read it aloud. We can bury the letter or safely burn it while remembering all the pain and happiness we experienced and consciously forgive our former partner, release them, and send our blessings to move on.

If we don't fully close the door on our past relationships mentally and emotionally, we can't fully open the door to our present relationship. It doesn't mean that we cannot speak to our former partner, especially if children are involved, but we can free ourselves of the emotional and energetic baggage that we may still be carrying.

14

COMPASSION

Compassion is an invaluable asset in any relationship. It requires seeing into the heart of another with an open heart and feeling their pain and suffering. It's through compassion that we come to understand our partner and care enough to want to support them. Every person has a history. For all the sweetness of life, there is also bitterness and pain. To truly understand our partner, we need to examine deep beneath the surface, and do so with compassion. Looking through the lens of compassion softens our reactions and our vision of our partner.

When you have compassion for your partner, as angry or hurt as you may be at a given moment, you can keep a loving perspective. Through compassion, the sense of your partner being an opponent falls away. You can see their wounds and help to heal them by treading gently around their pain rather than adding to it.

In the height of conflict, while we struggle with our own pain, we may fail to see that of our partner. We push to have ours acknowledged. It takes a lot of love, awareness, and strength to feel the distress of our partner in the midst of our own and care enough to want to reduce it.

Compassion requires us to be humble in order to not allow a feeling of superiority to blind our vision of our partner's pain. In this way, humility opens the door to a deeper relationship.

15

EMPOWERMENT

Every person wants to feel appreciated and valued. There are distinct ways in which we can uplift someone or, to the contrary, make them feel inferior. Sadly, we can waste a lot of our time fighting to maintain or increase our power by reducing someone else's. Driving a nail further into a post doesn't actually make the nail shorter than the next one, but it gives that illusion. In the same manner, we may disempower our partner only to boost our own self. People who disempower another are usually hurting within themselves, even though outwardly they show a façade of strength. If deep within, you feel inferior, your only weapon to cover your weakness is to reduce another's power. Yet, empowering one another can lift both parties higher, simultaneously increasing the happiness of the relationship. However, it has to be a two-way street; both partners must support each other in their needs and dreams and have compassion for each other's weakness and pain.

If we are not truly listening to each other, not honoring each other, not giving each other time or affection, not caring for each other's needs, and in addition deceiving each other, calling each other names, and making everything else more important than our partner, we are telling them that they are not important to us—hence disempowering them. However, we may not consider any of these actions as disempowering in the moment and we may whole-heartedly believe that they are justified.

Though mutually lifting one another up has optimal benefits in a relationship, it can be difficult to continuously empower someone who is disempowering you and making you feel inferior. Retaliating against disempowerment with the same treatment only creates a vicious cycle which spirals the relationship downward.

True empowerment is seeing the greatness of another. When we remember it's about being on the same team and sharing a vision, we can become more conscious of the actions we are taking to disempower our partner and make a decision to correct those actions. No one wants to feel they are a failure, a loser, or always wrong. Sometimes it's not what we do, but what we stop doing that actually turns a relationship around for the better. Lifting our partner through sincere compliments and words of gratitude, seeing the good in them, listening to them, spending quality time with them, and making them feel they are a priority in our life is what allows our relationship to soar higher. Choose to see the greatness in your partner.

The two wings of the bird work together
to rise to the sky and feel the joy of creation.

16

FORGIVENESS

Forgiveness can lead to freedom within. Everyone has hurt another, either unconsciously or consciously, in retaliation for pain we have experienced. When we hurt someone, it usually means we ourselves are hurting within. Fear and insecurity can bring out the worst in us. Through cultivating compassion, it becomes easier to find forgiveness in our hearts for someone who has hurt us.

We may believe that we have forgiven someone and moved on, but the true test of knowing whether we have truly forgiven them is when we can pray for them from the bottom of our heart and wish them happiness. It doesn't mean we forget what they have done nor allow it to happen again, but it does mean sincerely wishing them well, understanding their pain, and feeling free from the negative feelings we may be holding towards them.

To pray for someone who has hurt us requires both compassion and humility. Forgiveness softens our heart and frees it of the heavy weight of the pain we are carrying. Holding a grudge or having feelings of revenge may give us a false sense of power and entitlement, but the burden of grudge holding or revenge seeking gradually weighs us down even more than the pain. By throwing off the load and forgiving our partner, we lighten our own energy and heart to be able to love both ourselves and others more deeply.

17

PRAYER

Have you tried starting your day together with a prayer? The power of prayer is often underestimated. When we pray, it's not necessarily for our wishes and dreams to be answered by the divine; rather, it puts our mind and energy in the direction of our dreams.

It's difficult to manifest something or arrive at a destination if the path is unclear or if the wheels are not in motion. Through prayer, we can set the tone of our day with our partner. We have so much on our minds and so many responsibilities to deal with that we can get distracted from our shared vision.

In times of conflict, rather than giving each other the silent treatment and suffering in pain until one reaches out to the other again, we can pray for each other and send each other light and love. Prayer should not be with an attitude of being better than the other, but with the intention of increasing the love within the relationship.

If we spent more time praying for each other rather than hating each other, criticizing each other, and having negative thoughts and emotions towards each other, the world and our relationship would be transformed.

Having someone pray for us, especially on a regular basis, is the greatest gift we can receive. Sincere prayer, coming from a pure heart with pure love, is like a gentle breeze that is always behind our back, caressing and protecting us.

As a couple, praying together every day at the start of the morning or before bedtime can be a beautiful ritual.

Here is a sample prayer that you can do together. Feel free to personalize it by adding or deleting whatever you feel is necessary so that it suits your vision.

Dear God (or Divine Light),

Keep our hearts open to each other. Let your grace flow through our lives. Let your joy flow between us. Help me see my partner through your eyes. Let me see the good in my partner. Let me listen to my partner's heart today. Help me uplift my partner. Help me to be humble. Help me to communicate with love. Let my words be gentle. Let me tell my partner how much I love them today. Let our relationship flourish and grow. Let me put aside enough time for my partner. Let me treat my partner with respect and honor. Dear God (or Divine Light), bless and protect our relationship with your grace, with your love, with your happiness.

18

NATURE'S WISDOM

Among the indigenous people in South America, nature is sacred. Before asking for or taking anything from nature, an offering is always given. They follow the law of reciprocity. They believe we can't take anything for granted. Anyone or anything that gives of itself to us—whether it's their time, kindness, or resources—is bestowing a gift on us. We are not entitled to anything. Through this sense of humility and understanding, these people see life as an exchange of energies, and harmony is achieved through this balance. Anytime there is an imbalance in this exchange, we see it reflected in our life as well as in nature.

Apart from showing a deep sense of gratitude, this spirit of exchange also offers a deep respect towards life. If we carry this mindset into our relationships, we realize that we have so many expectations in life that we often fail to realize the gifts that are given to us.

Imagine waking up every morning and bowing down to your partner in thanks for their presence in your life. Imagine giving them a small acknowledgment of appreciation every single day. Imagine seeing them as a gift in your life rather than someone who is there to serve you. Imagine recognizing all that they give you as precious and something to be extremely grateful for. Imagine how drastically your perspective on each other and life would change!

The air that we breathe, the water that we drink, and the food we eat can all be taken away instantly. When we see all the wildfires, hurricanes, and other natural disasters which happen and how quickly a person can go from having everything to having nothing, from being alive to passing on, we need to recognize our deepest gratitude for all that we have—no matter whether we lead a life of luxury or a simple, humble one.

In times of emergency, we especially realize the value of our relationships. We are not entitled to relationships. They are a gift in our life to take care of and cherish, just as the sun, the moon, the earth, the trees, the waters, and our food are gifts.

The indigenous people understand their interdependence with nature and consequently give their respect at all times. In a fast-paced life, many lose this connection to nature, which is a reflection of their own inner being. We are all a part of nature. When we awaken that connection, we naturally begin to have respect for ourselves, for all of nature, and for the relationships with people in our lives.

Search deep within your soul
to find your treasure chest of love.
Open its lid and share generously.
Love only increases when it's shared.

19

~~~

COUPLE'S MEDITATION
WITH NATURE

This meditation can be done either together with your partner or by yourself. Find a comfortable place to sit or lay down and allow yourself to feel completely relaxed without any disturbance for at least ten minutes.

Imagine yourself and your partner sitting on a rock close to a tall, gentle waterfall cascading down in the middle of a nature setting. Your back is to the waterfall, and you feel the water gently spraying on your head and body, washing away your anger, fear, hatred, sadness, or jealousy. Allow this to continue for a few minutes while you imagine all the traumas and pain that you are carrying being cleansed by the warm, gentle waterfall.

As you feel yourself becoming lighter and more joyful, a gentle, warm wind brushes against your face and body. When you feel cleared of all the heavy energies within yourself and between you and your partner, see yourself moving to another rock that is dry, ahead of you.

Sit on this rock, listening to the waterfall behind you and feeling the sun shining in the sky and showering its light and warmth onto your entire body. Feel its rays filling your heart and entire body. Feel the peace and warmth within you.

Now imagine an emerald green light surrounding both you and your partner. See the light encompassing both of you, entering into your hearts, and filling you with its power, love, and beauty.

Filled with peace, love, lightness, and strength, take your partner's hand and feel the love flowing between you.

When you feel complete, thank the waterfall and the sun for helping you to heal the discord between you and bow down to them in gratitude.

.

20

WE

As long as one partner sees themselves as a single, independent person separate from the other, conflict is guaranteed in a relationship. The idea of relationship necessitates coming into unity with another and seeing each other as a team, not as opponents. Seeing each other as one does not mean losing our sense of self and letting go of our own needs. Rather, it is taking not only ourselves into consideration but also our partner and the relationship as a whole.

In reality, there are three entities in any relationship: you, your partner, and your relationship. What is the purpose of a relationship? It is to come together and form a union towards a similar vision. We not only need to consider what is best for our own self, but also what is best for the other and the relationship as a whole. When we develop the "we" consciousness in a relationship, the chances of success increase. It is with this mindset that wanting to make the other happy, true listening, honesty, loyalty, compassion and forgiveness become natural desires, and communication can lead to solutions rather than arguments.

A person who is focused on doing what they want, without any concern for others, can be fine leading the single life. But if they are in a relationship and do not take into consideration the impact that their decisions have on their partner and family, challenges will inevitably arise, especially if the outcomes of their decisions are hurtful to those loved ones.

In a relationship, everything that we do will ultimately reverberate to the other. All the decisions that we make will affect our partner as well as ourselves. If we gain or lose money, it will impact our partner. If we fall ill, it will impact our partner. If we are extremely stressed, it will impact our partner. Our highs and lows, joys and sorrows, gains and losses, will all ripple into our partner's life; therefore, important decisions and plans must be considered together, as a team, to allow the garden of the relationship to grow in its beauty.

What can you do to foster the "we" mindset in your relationship?

21

~~∮~~

HEALTHY CHOICES

Life evolves based on the choices that we make. Every day we are making choices that will either bring us closer in our relationship or create distance.

It can be difficult to discern which of our choices are moving us closer or further apart, especially when emotions are involved. In moments of discomfort and challenge, we may lose sight of the goal with our partner and take actions or respond to circumstances in ways that distance us, though that is not what we ultimately desire.

Through making healthy choices, we have a greater chance of success in our relationship. The healthy choices discussed thus far in this book are the winds that take your sails towards a destination of union and love in your relationship.

When we start our day with prayer or meditation we put our minds towards choosing love over power so that we can make healthy choices throughout the day. The more we bring ourselves into alignment with nature and foster inner harmony, the more harmony we can create in our relationship.

What are healthy choices that we can make? Let's summarize:

- Choose to seek love over power.
- Think about what you can give more than what you can get.
- Remember the law of reciprocity.
- Water the plant of your relationship with your sincere presence, affection, and quality time.
- Listen from your heart, giving your full attention. Let the words you hear enter your being.

- Choose your words and silence consciously.
- Speak the truth to bring you closer. Lies create walls.
- Develop greater focus to maintain loyalty.
- Reflect on your habits in dealing with conflict and make better choices.
- Clear the weeds of unfinished energies of the past.
- See each other through the eyes of compassion.
- Empower each other.
- Forgive in order to free yourself.
- Pray for each other and your relationship daily.
- Meditate with nature to bring your heart into alignment and clear heavy energies.
- Live in gratitude and respect for what your partner is giving you.
- See each other as a team, as "we," rather than opponents.

The divine is in everything—
in the breezes at night, in the rays of the sun,
in the waves of the ocean, in the trees standing tall,
in the earth beneath our feet,
in the eyes of each other.

Wishing you the strength of heart and mind to make healthy choices that lead you to the deepest love, joy, and harmony in your relationships.

May this book guide you in your journey to create a garden that blossoms with the beauty of open hearts. Whenever you are faced with a difficult moment, open this book to any chapter to remind yourself of what it takes to see the garden of your dreams bear fruit. Take it one day at a time and you will surely reach the harmony and love that you long for in your relationships.

With love,

Rita Panahi, L.Ac.

Stay Connected

www.facebook.com/RitaPanahiAuthor

www.facebook.com/groups/RitaPanahiAuthor

@RitaPanahiAuthor

@RitaAuthor

www.ritapanahi.com

www.author.ritapanahi.com

ABOUT THE AUTHOR

Rita Panahi, L.Ac., Dipl.O.M., holds a master's in Chinese Medicine, a five thousand-year-old medicine. In her practice, she sees how powerfully the relationships of her clients affect their physical health and overall well-being and supports them in their healing process. In addition, she has trained for over twenty-five years with indigenous healers, among whom divorce and separation are extremely rare, learning about their dynamic relationship with nature and its reflection in their lives. She combines their understanding and professional experience she has gained over the decades into this book *Simple Relationship Wisdom: Secrets to a Happy Relationship*, wishing to inspire others to build healthier and more harmonious relationships and lives.

ALSO BY RITA PANAHI, L.AC.

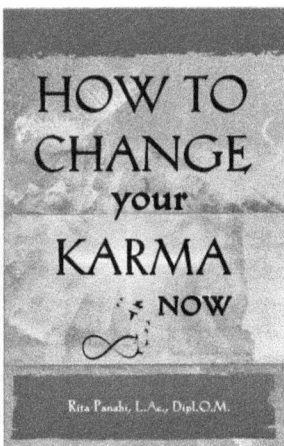